Mentoring Startup Entrepreneurs Part III

The Mentor Diaries

I0472768

Dhananjay Parkhe
Vol. 1, Part III, 1st Edition

Table of Contents

Introduction to Mentoring Startup Entrepreneur Part III

We need and meet several specialist Mentors in our life time as Startups, Entrepreneurs and C-Level Executives. I feel blessed that I have met them when most needed.

The Dictionary meaning of Mentor is

Mentor: गुरू (Guru - a wise and trusted guide and advisor) The verbs are Mentored: mentored Mentoring: मॉनिटरींग (Do Monitoring) Mentors: मार्गदर्शन (Show a Path) In Marathi it means सल्लागार (Advisor) गुरू (Guru) Someone who participates in a Council-serve as a teacher or trusted counselor).

The different ways the word Mentor is used gives you a clear idea of what a Mentor stands for/ What he does or does not do.

For e.g.

1. "It's a tale of the teacher mentor and student who learn from each other, but only in part." Back to Back Mentor
2. "He was her friend and mentor until his death." – Life Time Mentor.
3. "Back in Rome, he met Polybius, who became his friend and his mentor in preparing him for a public career." Career Mentor.
4. "He was a great mentor and friend and he will be sadly missed by everyone who was lucky enough to know him well." Friend, Philosopher and Guide Mentor.
5. "There is also a new mentor program linking young people to adults to develop positive relationships outside their peer group." Ice Breaker Mentor.
6. "But finding a guide, a coach, a friend, a mentor and a support unit, all wrapped up in the one person, is not going to be easy." Composite Mentor.
7. "His father is more than a customer, however, serving as a mentor and adviser to Daly. "Customer Mentor
8. "The latter was his mentor and friend, for whose editorial skills he always retained sincere admiration." Look Up to Mentor.
9. "It will not even allow me to say that I have been the best mentor and example for students, but I have always tried to be." Idol Mentor.
10. "He was very encouraging and since then he has become a mentor and friend." Affirmation Mentor.
11. "After four sessions with his mentor, the student was able to pass the course." Tutor Mentor.

12. "He became my mentor and good friend and he was one of the world's great authorities on … "Authority Mentor"
13. "Under the terms of the Trust, a mentor is to be provided for the successful students to assist and support them during their time at college." Official Mentor"
14. "She's a very dear friend and a great mentor and I really look up to her." Peer Mentor
15. "He was a kind, gracious, and generous friend, and a mentor beyond compare. "He was her friend and mentor until his death in 1915. Forever Mentor.
16. "He is our mentor, our guide, and he possesses an intellect the size of a planet". Advisor Mentor.
17. "As the report describes, the mentor program has contributed to the career advancement of protégés' ". Performance Mentor
18. "A good mentor can help a student or practitioner sort through the options and make decisions". Manage Mentor.

Getting Started

Sharing some of the types of mentors and Gurus I came across in my lifetime and in my Entrepreneurship journey. I developed an inimitable style of using Humor bordering on Satire to explain and drive home his point of view. The list of mentors is not exhaustive; these are just the mentors I have come across at different stages of his life and entrepreneurial journey.

He is a firm believer in the Buddhist saying "When the Pupil is Ready, the Master Appears. "In his 43 years of working and entrepreneurial career he was blessed to have had the Best of Mentors to help him at different times.

Chapter Number 1
Who is the Right Mentor for you?
Choice of Mentors

While I believe in the Buddhist saying "The Master appears when the Pupil is ready" – I also believe that an Entrepreneur, a C-Level Executive must be forever alert and keep looking for New Mentors to help them with knowledge, wisdom, path finding at different stages of their Business, Enterprise, Working life journey

I have described in few statements in the Introduction about the various Labels I have chosen to give to different mentors for ease of understanding of the readers. You may agree or disagree with them and choose what suites you once you have understood the essence of the reason WHY you need a mentor and WHO should be your mentor for WHAT purpose.

I have shared below some of my personal experiences of finding the right mentors and about some mentors who found me or they were assigned to me at the workplace.

We also discuss some of the useful stories of Success and failures and where Mentors appeared to show the right path to people/ entrepreneurs/ C-Level Executives at the right time.

Chapter Number 2
Back to Back Mentor
Choice of Mentors

"It's a tale of the teacher mentor and student who learn from each other, but only in part." Back to Back Mentor.

It may sound strange but it is true. The Secrecy maintained in MNC's and Global Corporations about Senior people joining is phenomenal. I was recruited quietly and sent for an induction to a Region where the Regional team was sworn to secrecy as they were to quietly induct me in the company and this was even without the knowledge of the HR Director/ Head at that time. There was a reason to it. I was to replace a non-performer who was a Profit Centre head and if known it could have caused problems and there was to be an element of surprise in this succession plan.

I went to this region. I was from the industry and had also run same business as a Profit Centre Head/ Generalist at my own and another company at national level but they were indigenous companies and to that extent their processes/ policies were bit rudimentary and not fully mature as a corporate. The Regional Profit center head was a close friend from another company where we worked together and hence there was no resistance from the team.

All appointments were quietly taken, including operations at night, airport duties at odd hours and listening to the customer service function and customer handling quietly from a cabin were all great. The rub came when I sat with the Regional Sales Head. He was a Star Performer and a tough internal competitor in the Regional Best competitions. He was apprehensive to give out too much (but Official mentor status was thrust on him). He was aggressive but not abrasive, he was tough and polite, he was firm but not a stickler for rules and policies – but was unwilling to share the secret ways of Winning regional internal competitions by slightly bending rules here and there.

Fortunately for me, I had 4 such juniors equally experienced and qualified, mature and performers in my prior company so I decided to share transparently the secret ways my Regional Sales Heads would act in similar or difficult situations and how they would still make the numbers against all odds without bending rules but seeking concessions officially! This was different to my New Mentor. Instead of the normal 2 hours our session lasted nearly 6 hours between smoking and coffee breaks and went Back to Back. My mentor then told his boss and my close friend that 'The session went well. It was Back to Back – a great learning experience!' to which my friend gave a knowing smile (as if saying I told you so").

Sometimes we are lucky in the onboarding process of a new company to find such great mentors who know all the tricks, all the ways of playing the game, all the rules and how to read between the lines. It worked for me.

It also helped me nearly a decade later of playing the role of the Country Integrity Chief or the conscience keeper / Disciplinary committee Head. The Whistleblower / fraud investigating team would bring up a plan of investigation and by function I could show them the path, discuss the wily and naïve ways of how people bend rules. In over 400+ investigations we could find proof and confessions 100% ☺.

The true value of back to back mentoring is in Radical Transparency and generation of Trust between two individuals which leads to sharing and develops mutual respect towards each other.

Chapter Number 3
The Life Time Mentor
Choice of Mentors

"He was her friend and mentor until his death." – Life Time Mentor.

Many of you may have heard the story of the starfish on the beach. It is a great illustration of the essence of "making-a-difference" by a mentor. I quite like this story and hence sharing with the readers again.

One fine morning one man was walking along the beach. It was a great sight, watching the ocean waves breaking on the shore, he noticed a most unusual phenomenon. The beach was already littered with thousands of starfish that had been washed up on the shore and were now dying in the sun.

Not very far down the beach in the distance he could see a young woman picking up the starfish and throwing them back in to the ocean, one at a time.

When he was close enough to be heard above the roar of the waves the man said: "You're wasting your time. There are thousands of starfish here. You can't possibly make any difference!"

The young woman reached down, picked up a starfish, and then threw it as far as she could back into the sea. "I made a difference to that one," she said, reaching down to pick up another.

Whether we are mentoring a colleague or a young person, a student or a budding entrepreneur, a peer Director or upcoming C Suite mentor - the impact we can make will be that of the woman saving starfish – truly life-changing.

Mentoring thus, never became a business for me, nor it is a Money-Spinner wheel. For me it is a fulfillment of Personal Social Responsibility, my way of Giving Back to the Society which gave me so much in life. There is just one caveat, I choose and decide the Coach-ability or otherwise (to coach or not to coach) of the Mentee/ Coached. About that, in some other article, some day! ☺

Chapter Number 4
Career Mentor
Choice of Mentors

I read this quote about Polybius - "Back in Rome, he met Polybius, who became his friend and his mentor in preparing him for a public career." Career Mentor.

Mentorship is a personal developmental relationship in which a more experienced or more knowledgeable person helps to guide a less experienced or less knowledgeable person. However, true mentoring is more than just answering occasional questions or providing ad hoc help. It is about an ongoing relationship of learning, dialogue, and challenge.

The person in receipt of mentorship may be referred to as a protégé(male), a protégée (female), an apprentice or, in recent years, a mentee.

"Mentoring" is a process that always involves communication and is relationship based, but its precise definition is elusive. One definition of the many that have been proposed, is

"Mentoring is a process for the informal transmission of knowledge, social capital, and the psychosocial support perceived by the recipient as relevant to work, career, or professional development; mentoring entails informal communication, usually face-to-face and during a sustained period of time, between a person who is perceived to have greater relevant knowledge, wisdom, or experience (the mentor) and a person who is perceived to have less (the protégé".

Polybius in the quote above is thought to take its name from that of the Greek historian Polybius, who was known for his assertion that historians should never report what they cannot verify through interviews with witnesses. In the succeeding years, Polybius resided in Rome, completing his historical work while occasionally undertaking long journeys through the Mediterranean countries in the furtherance of his history, with the aim of obtaining firsthand knowledge of historical sites.

He apparently interviewed veterans to clarify details of the events he was recording and was similarly given access to archival material.
Little is known of Polybius' later life; he most likely accompanied Scipio to Spain, acting as his military advisor during the Numantine War.

A key theme of his book *The Histories* is the good statesman as virtuous and composed. The character of the Polybian statesman is exemplified in that of Philip II. His beliefs about Philip's character led Polybius to reject historian Theopompus' description of Philip's private, drunken debauchery.

For Polybius, it was inconceivable that such an able and effective statesman could have had an immoral and unrestrained private life as described by Theopompus." From Wikipedia.

In recounting the Roman Republic, Polybius stated that "the Senate stands in awe of the multitude, and cannot neglect the feelings of the people".

A Career Mentor like Polybius taught several important lessons:

1. Personal Verification of events should be done fact finding by interviews.
2. Good statesman is virtuous and composed.
3. It is inconceivable that an able and effective statesman could have an immoral and unrestrained private life.
4. The Senate stands in awe of the multitude, and cannot neglect the feelings of the people.

Chapter Number 5
Friend, Philosopher, Guide
Choice of Mentors

"He was a great mentor and friend and he will be sadly missed by everyone who was lucky enough to know him well." Friend, Philosopher, Guide Mentor.

The lucky ones in life either find out or get found out by the Right Mentors who become their Friends, Philosophers and Guides. I was lucky to have found at least 3 such individuals and they all happened to be my Bosses at different companies and became mentors by choice.

C Suite Mentoring involves High Stake Decision Making and the Mentoring helps to equip Mentee to take Better and still better decisions.

My mentor walked me thru the three critical steps – Hand-holding initially till I had acquired Self-Assurance; inspiring and provoking me to compete with my worthy colleagues in internal competitions and focusing Outward at the competition – combining the two steps – Significance and Strategic direction. These were invaluable lessons

1. Self-Assurance - someone who remains true to his/her beliefs, judgements and is confident of his/her ability

2. Significance - someone who seeks to do something significant and recognized by others for this

3. Strategic – someone who can foresee a clear direction through the complexity of a situation

My first boss and mentor in the bank was a tough Chartered Accountant who would say to me "You can make as many mistakes as you wish – knowingly and unknowingly and I shall point them to you. If you repeat them… you'll invoke may Anger which is just one word away from DANGER ☺ ". YES. He was an Angry Mentor as I was a slow learning pupil at times. The lesson was invaluable.

My second mentor boss was in the fertilizer company who taught me to be "Scrupulous and Meticulous" and 'Religiously' follow the instruction set and the check lists. Once when I met with a Bike accident – his first question was "Did you follow the Vehicle check list". Second "Did you fill up the Accident reporting form correctly?". He was a Gem of a person and a great human being.

My third boss and mentor and I worked for the longest duration together. He knew my character and my off/ On attention spans and constantly goaded me to do Projects. Mostly improvement projects for saving costs, improving efficiency, cost cutting etc. He also judged my aptitude and began giving me Inside OUT opportunities to represent my company in business forums, government delegations, committees and public affairs. He then would ask me to use Outside IN and use the connections made for improving business. Wonderful lessons. One of the unforgettable learning was "Never take a loan for buying a depreciating Asset". He was a Chartered Accountant too.

It is rare to be found out by Mentors who have in them the strong ability to mentor others. They make the best Friends, Philosophers and Guides for the C-Level aspirants and Mentor them to their desired position.

Chapter Number 6

Ice-Breaker Mentor
Choice of Mentors

There is also a new mentor program linking young people to adults to develop positive relationships outside their peer group." Ice Breaker Mentor.

The best lesson I learnt thru a HR training program was APPRECIATIVE ENQUITY and the best lesson from Dr. Marshall Goldsmith – ACCOUNTABILITY PARTNER. You can read about the latter on his website and in his bestseller books.

As an Ice-Breaker Mentor I had an opportunity in the MNC to become part of a team of Global Assessors for Fast Track Program for Young Executives. We began the program by visiting Business Schools for Placement Interviews. Post recruitment and onboarding the Management Trainees would work in the specialist department of their strength for a year or two viz., Finance, Marketing, Sales, Accounts, Operations, Credit Control, Audit etc. They would then go for an Online Assessment test which was held globally on the company Intranet and the Global Assessors would then make online Assessment, write feedback, Give Ratings and have personal interviews with people who were in the Top 5 from different countries. The final shortlist of about 15 would then go thru two rounds of personal interviews with the Global hierarchy of management and finally 6 were chosen for the CEO interview. Only 3 would be taken each year for the Fast track program initially – later this number increased. Selected candidates would work with Global Functional Heads One per Head for a duration of 1 to 3 years and then could either become a Country Director for the function or a Country Head itself.

They would do projects, presentations both internal and external and would continue to be in touch with One Global Mentor each who would do debriefing, handle any of their issues and make introductions for them if they required cross functional support.

It worked. Many young executives attained Global positions of their choosing and did well.

The Ice Breaker Mentor helps open doors for the Mentee within the organization, reduces the resistance by his awe of position and influence as also with his persuasive nature. APPRECIATIVE ENQUIRY helps when there is a conflict between two hotheads who do not see eye to eye and are otherwise constantly at loggerheads and openly airing their differences to any willing listeners. We have all seen them they exist in all organizations.

Having a Positive energy channelizing plan like the fast track program can help as also the Appreciative Enquiry kind of intervention coupled with hard counselling works wonders.

Chapter Number 7

Composite Mentor

Mid-Career crisis and Choice of Mentors

"But finding a guide, a coach, a friend, a mentor and a support unit, all wrapped up in the one person, is not going to be easy."

Search the right Mentor – A Generalist may seem to be the answer but what you may need is an accomplished COMPOSITE MENTOR who is senior and mature yet has time on hands to help and Mentor you.

I am reminded of a story of my ex colleague. He was a Sales Head of a Region had background in Merchant Banking with a MNC bank. He lost his job due to a Harassment complaint.

He repented and came to me to seek advice. He was looking for a job. Protection of salary and position was important than being a MNC or equivalent. He joined a furniture company specializing in Corporate Chairs, ergonomically designed Chairs, Very high backed, Very high priced Chairs. In the Indian Capital – if you had the data base and the aggressive drive and social connections – doors easily open for you. My friend did very well in this business so much so, the company owner felt threatened and sued him on phony charges. While the case was, my friend was also asked to leave the company.

He met me again two years after the first meeting, facing a mid-career crisis and in search of a job again. My suggestion was to be an Entrepreneur if it motivates him. I asked him questions to him about the Furniture industry, trends, innovations, market size, his Roll-O-Desk cards, leads he could generate, financial capacity and risk willingness. He was keen as he had enough of bosses and wanted to enter BOOM – Being One's Own Man phase in life.

We met couple of times, discussed and he did some research in India and Far East countries where he could source Furniture. He also used his Roll O Desk and found one of the leading Architects of India who was designing Call Centers in few towns for MNCs and Indian companies. He was in search of Good, economical, ergonomically designed chairs for the staff – not the very expensive variety. He was the person responsible for creating the tender and approving items without tender too.

My friend sourced these chairs and after few iterations, modifications and supplier Logistics and pricing negotiations won his first order. He met me next year in January. He wanted me to set his Goal in this One-Person Company which he operated out of his briefcase, a brick like Motorola mobile (1997) and a Car. He said he is now driving a new car, has the new mobile with International Roaming (which was hugely expensive to have in those years) and a Very expensive branded watch which showed two countries' timings ☺ (I jokingly said to him that don't two time your spouse ☺). He had begun to taste success. We set his first-year target as 50 Million Rupees and a simple profit goal after expenses and the Architect's commission and he met me again a year later saying 'Boss I have overachieved – I have done 100 million Rupees business last year so set my Goal again. We set it ambitiously at 250 Million Rupees after discussing the ongoing projects, the feedback on chairs by users / Quality control / returns/ repairs etc. and knew it was achievable as the Supplier maintained excellent quality control. This brought him terrific credibility and for this Top Architect my friend was the sole Chair supplier. He met me 2 years later – invited me to his new Bungalow, showed me his High-priced car, collection of the watches and new mobiles and said I continue to operate out of a briefcase and have no employees. I have a computer at home and a Tally accounting system and I have a lawyer and Chartered Accountants who keep consulting me about business/ taxation/ regulation aspects. Business was good and so was life.

For this friend "But finding a guide, a coach, a friend, a mentor and a support unit, all wrapped up in the one person, is not going to be easy." Who chose me as a guide, a coach and mentor and above all a support system and friend – I became a Trusted person. From his down days to where he had reached it was a tough journey but fortunately the Elements / Ingredients of business success came together. His own perseverance, hard work and business acumen finally helped. I moved town but we kept in touch – he progressed well but remained a ONE-PERSON COMPANY – An Entrepreneur.

Chapter Number 8

"Customer Mentor".

Choice of Mentors

"He is more than a customer, however, serving as a mentor and adviser to me. "Customer Mentor".

Let us understand the difference between often interchangeably misused terms like, Coach, Mentor, Advisor and Consultant.

Coach/Executive Coach

The coach works with an entrepreneur/ startup to help them improve performance; of leadership, business, or personal. In all the cases, they are structured to assist achievement of goals, understand and resolve challenges, and focus on growth. The coach is neither Omniscient – all knowing or Omnipotent- all powerful. The entrepreneur may seek nor does the work on behalf of their customers, but brings an outside-in and unemotional perspective. Coaches know how to take an entrepreneur through a process of discovery and skill development, asking questions to lead their customer to their desired achievements. The benefits of the coaching engagement are measured by the performance of the entrepreneur and/or his company. The customer attains better capability attains business growth.

One of my customers gave me an insight / insider view about their buying decision making process and equipped me with better competitor analysis, comparative tables/ charts of Features/ Benefits and Advantages and come well prepared for Objection handling/ Negotiation and Closing of Sale.

Mentor

A mentor relationship is for long-term benefit. This happens by deep knowledge about each other. Mentors' relationship can be termed as customer intimacy and it is personal because of time spent together, transparent sharing of interactions, honest intentions, mutual caring. Mentors are safe connections who take on the task of developing mentees, and have no agenda. They are freely share knowledge and experience. Mentoring is Free while Coaching, Consulting and Advisors are not. Unless Advisors choose to go Pro-Bono! My work with Startups as Accelerator is not short term and therefore I am quite choosy about whom to take on board as Mentee and the customer who became my Mentor remained a customer even when I had nothing to sell to him having changed companies. He was a specialist in his field and liked Mentoring and was very choosy.

Consultant

A consultant is described as an individual or company who we hire to do something or bring new knowledge, ideas, changes, processes to improve and contribute to business. Their resources, knowledge, or experience can supplement our efforts. A consultant is not interested in our personal development, performance or skills but they use theirs to accomplish tasks or reach goals instead of us. We get the work done without our having to lift a finger. My customer taught me the value of time, time management, maintaining time-sheets for tasks performed and being able to quote an hourly rate for my consulting expertise.

Advisor

The Advisor is a trouble-shooter, sharp-shooter - someone with specialist expertise or experience who helps us in a special way. They do so for a fee, or as part of a more formal advisory role or group, or as a favor or for in-kind services, sometimes they go totally Pro-Bono if it is a social activity which they are themselves passionate about as their own 'Giving back to Society' mission. The relationship is more casual than the other three described here. You ask questions and they have answers. They listen a little and talk a lot, can help an entrepreneur get an urgent problem understood and solved quickly. In my life-time some of my customers offered me their specialist advice as a 'quid pro quo' to solve my problem and what they wanted in return in price terms was very low but was an invaluable learning lesson for me. One needs a listening skill extraordinary to deal with customers especially when they are specialists and can be your Advisors.

Chapter Number 9

Look up to Mentor

Choice of Mentors

"He was his mentor and friend, for whose editorial skills he always retained sincere admiration." Look Up to Mentor.

I am talking here about a Junior or a Peer / a colleague in another department or your own who impresses you with his/ her skills and is available to make a long-term friendship relationship which at times goes beyond and is valued as a Mentor relationship.

When I was struggling to come out of Entrepreneurship which was failing and due to poor management of scarce finances and two large customers declaring bankruptcy I was looking for a way out one of my old colleague called.

He invited me to be his guest for couple of days in another town and I stayed in a hotel. We were together for almost all the time discussing till the wee hours of morning trying to find a way out – whether to continue the losing business, or look for a job. Finally, together we reached a decision that I must quit the business I am losing money in and begin looking for employment.

He shared with me a home truth then. He said, failed entrepreneurs are not the best in demand in a Corporate world especially MNC! Second, at my life stage (I was in mid 40's) it is difficult to get employment in a company unless they have a need to get someone from outside (as against home-grown timber) and if I have three people inside that company who can be my Referees and vouch for me totally!

Over a period of next few months we interacted over phone regularly and met couple of times. We finally found that his company may need someone with my ability/ experience but it would need a hard-sell inside by three or four of my ex colleagues/ friends who also worked there for me to convince the new CEO to recruit me.

My friend had the relationship skills, negotiating skills and he almost did 50% of my job before I could go for the first personal interview. The HR Head rejected as expected "A failed entrepreneur, on the brink of bankruptcy and has no dress sense" was a great Feedforward and learning – a reality check for me which only a true friend and mentor can have the courage to tell me on my face. The intent was indeed to help me. This is an invaluable experience of life. Unforgettable. I could not afford a Bright new white shirt – leave alone a Suit and I had forgotten to wear a tie in my 3 years of Entrepreneurship! Such Mentors are very rare to come by in life.

Chapter Number 10

Idol/Icon Mentor

Choice of Mentors

"He won't even allow me to say that he has been my best mentor and example for students, as he has always tried to be." Humble Mentor.

I went back to a B-School for an Evening Part-time Management Diploma course and ended up doing Marketing Management One year course as a Topper. I then went for a two-year Business Management course which I did not finish the last semester as I had landed a job which had 20-25 days' travel. I joined this course 14 years after my post-graduation. I met two most valuable mentors at the Institute. But about them sometime later.

I joined an Independent Directors' Course 17 years. This was a short-term part time evening course to get certified as Non-Executive Director. I met the mentor about whom I wrote above as a Humble Mentor.

He was an Independent Director with Several companies himself – all Blue Chip, all Richest in India. He was one of the first Founder Partner of the Big 4 Audit firms in the world and a very polished gentleman who was an expert extraordinary in his subject. Most humble and not very easily accessible in the first instance – he taught us the value and importance of 'Arm's length relationship' in business.

He had a great flair for English language and he would explain the jargon in very simple and easy language for even a novice to understand because of the everyday life examples he would use.

We passed the course and went our ways thanking all our teachers and professors for the knowledge they imparted and waited for us to be invited to become Independent Directors for which there was projected to be huge need in India.

I chanced to meet in Bangalore for an Independent Directors' day-long session which was Chaired by (now defunct) an Airlines' CFO. On my table, was a Senior Headhunter whose card read 'Board Practice' rather famously! ☺

I met our teacher during a break and said that even after 4 years – no offers came my way. He asked me what he thought of the Airline and the CFO Chairing the function. I knew – there is no escaping! I must have to be truthful, cogent, frank and honest. I said to him "Sir, I am doubtful and bit skeptical!" As if affirming, something he also believed – he said to me "Remember, I taught you to keep your Resignation letter always in your upper pocket, just in case – when you are an Independent Director? "I said, Yes Sir!". He then gave me one of his famous lessons from Audit firm, consulting firm and nearly 50 years of experience of dealing with the 'Rich and Famous' the Who's Who of Indian Corporates – He said "When in doubt, just learn to say a very firm and polite NO! AND you will never fail!" He said, "Your first instinct may be always Right and follow it". As it turned out, few years later the Airline became defunct their founder an absconder a fugitive with Indian law and I remembered this Humble Mentor. He would not allow us to call or write to him as best Teacher/ Mentor but he gave some important lessons which were invaluable.

Chapter Number 11

Affirmation/ Positive Mentor

Choice of Mentors

"He was very encouraging and since then he has become a mentor and friend."
Affirmation Mentor.

Many a times, I meet youngsters and Entrepreneurs with few years of experience coming to me for advice. When I tell them whether they are looking for a Decision Support or a Decision itself – usually they are unclear.

I then do a brief probe, a harsh probe. I realize that they are Positive people. They are rational, they are adults – they can make decisions for them, they also do not wish to take my support for deciding. What they are looking for is just a simple affirmation that they decision they are taking is Right and it will work.

These decisions are sometimes simple, sometimes complex. Sometimes Ethical requiring them a reminder about using their own conscience. Sometimes these are People related, sometimes about major diversification, investment, shifts = a variety of decisions which Entrepreneurs/ Executives need to take.

They have done the Data gathering, Analyzed the Data, Got the Information, Processed the information, Got Facts, arranged their facts and then synthesized the Facts and reached options. They have filtered the options and finally reached two options from which to choose. Their mind sometimes says something, emotion pulls towards another, they like Option 1 but Wife, partner, friend or an old man in the family suggest the Option 2. They come to reconfirm, reassure with my support that the Option 1 which they have chosen will work - all they need is a pat on the back for following the process, following logic, reasoning, mind's processes and not allowing the emotions/sentiments to sway them from their path.

A word of Affirmation from the Mentor is all they are looking for and they usually get it unless they have done some fundamental error which I as a mentor can point out and ask them to go back to decision making process with the new approach – that has rarely happened.

Chapter Number 12

Tutor Mentor
Choice of Mentors

"After four sessions with his mentor, the student was able to pass the course." Tutor Mentor.

Entrepreneurs, Startups or C-Level executives who come to meet me are not appearing for any school, college or certification examination. So, they do not come for such advice to me. For such a need, there are Tutor Mentors as I call them. For e.g. a business needs Quality, Health and Safety or such other Certifications – I send them to find the right/ appropriate people who can take them thru the process.

If they have a Compliance, legal hurdle, the best course is to send them to a lawyer or someone who can take them thru the process and help with the compliance matters, legal hurdles.

If they have Taxation, Accounting, Audit related matters where they are stuck – it is best to send them to an expert in these matters.

I was and am a Generalist. At workplace from a Sales Manager I graduated to being a General Manager, Profit Centre Head and I was lucky to have had the support of very efficient, expert and knowledgeable functional heads. We cannot be a Know-all.

We should not try or pose to be what we are not. Perhaps the Mentees / Protégé's find me trustworthy because I tell them point blank that while I may suggest you a solution to your problem out of my hat (experience) I would still recommend you to visit the Expert/ Specialist who can give you the right solution. Very much like the General Practitioner Doctor who recommends us to visit a Specialist / Expert better qualified than him and saves our lives.

Chapter Number 13

Authority / Specialist Mentor
Choice of Mentors
"He became my mentor and good friend and he was one of the great authorities on
...,,,,,,,,"Authority Mentor

Who loves Doctors? Most people don't, unless they are their own father, mother, uncles, kith or kin. From the childhood we are frightened to meeting the Doctors especially the fright of bitter medicines, injections and we learn to hate the hospital smell, signet of blood, wounds etc. Some people may be different and may like and be friends with their Doctors.

I am one of them. Some of my good friends from 30-35 years ago are Doctors – either they were neighbors or became friends as we shared some good/ bad moments - - moments of pain, grief or joy together.

A close Doctor friend is now retired but was first a Civil Surgeon in a Government District Hospital and later became a practitioner and surgeon very famous in the entire district for his skill and treatment of the patients. I learnt how he treats and 'TREATS' the patients – which was with compassion, respect and empathy. This was a great trait and when I joined the MNC I often quoted him to my customer service staff in their trainings that an irate client for whom the service has failed – needs a TREATMENT with kid gloves, listening with empathy and compassion as if the suffering is yours too and you will bat for him with the company. It was useful.

Specialists like this doctor and others invest a lot of their time, money, efforts in learning and passing the course. They intern and work very hard thru shifts before they begin to learn to deal with patients on their own. One of my friends is a Mentor,

Guide and a Turn-Key consultant to fresh doctors ready to set up practice. He tells me that Doctors make very good friends. They learn business acumen the hard way but they follow the Process meticulously and scrupulously. They consult seniors if they are stuck or go back to books and journals for updating. My friend helps them commercially – he does things which Doctors cannot and are not allowed to do for e.g. Marketing and Promotion. He joins the business as partner, does Doctor/Potential patient meets informally, arranges talks on the specialty of the doctor, gets his other friend doctors as panelists and tells about the new clinic/ polyclinic coming up. He also erects Kiosks in the nearby Gardens early in the morning and arranges free medical checkups e.g. BP, Sugar, Eyes etc. and creates community awareness near the new Doctors' practice area. It helps.

Chapter Number 14

Official Mentor/ Executive Coach
Choice of Mentors
"Under the terms of the Trust, a mentor / Executive Coach is to be provided for the successful Executives to assist and support them during their time at company."
Official Mentor

I have my strong humble opinions about them but more about that a bit later. We discuss two types here:

1. External Mentor / Peer mentor
2. External Executive Coach / Peer Coach

While the External Mentors / Executive Coaches are typically very expensive many good companies often fell for the glib/smooth pitch/ sales talk and the fancy instruments of assessing behavior which some of them bring to the table. Personally, I have mixed experiences with them and have strong opinions. Strong, because rather than doing their role which is to help Executive improve Performance – they indulge in mudslinging, backbiting and politicking of the worst kind and get thrown out once a strong undercurrent forms and they get found out. Some HR heads also roll in the process who buy their merchandise and at times the CEO him/herself who become their Bhakts/ devotees and promote their books or freely distribute (charging the bill to company of course). This rarely helps. The reason for failure are also No Accountability either for Policy / Procedure and least for the Results with the result the External mentor and Executive is very detached and behave in matter-of-factly which is very impersonal and does not build any relationship.
I did have One Executive Coach who was different from what I described but One in 37 years of Career? You know what I mean!

The Internal Mentor/ Peer Coach has its limitations too. In the chapter on Back to Back mentor I briefly touched upon this. I was appointed a Peer Coach to two Directors who had come on board recently. The CEO wanted me to Peer Coach them and their teams. I made 3 different visits to meet them and their Direct Reports teams and realized that

They are 'Ún-coachable'. Not only were the sessions taken casually, the conversation back to back and trying to prove "One-Upmanship" that I decided to give up the effort. While one of them still made to a COO level but did not last 6 months in the company. Another left the company to become a COO in a private firm but last I heard, he was still in the job market. Unless there is a mutual respect these efforts do not work. And hence, I have a firm belief that Official Mentor / Official Executive Coach are the least needed initiatives HR Departments should never suggest.

Chapter Number 15

Peer Mentor
Choice of Mentors

"She's a very dear friend and a great mentor and I really look up to her." Peer Mentor.

She is not appointed by HR as your mentor, she is someone you look up to for support and guidance. She has a career path which you would like to follow and climb the hierarchy ladder as a new comer, junior in the company.

The reason is the person is friendly. Willing to listen to you and help you wade thru some of the known Corporate troubles, problems on the job which she has herself faced.

She is like a person who has passed thru a Jungle all alone. Got bruised, had cuts, got bitten by animals but waded thru and made a small path by regularly going to and fro. Over a period this new ground that she broke became a Kuccha village road which many crossed with or without help from her. More and more people travelled the road widened and animals, animal driven carts passed. Someone made it a Concrete road later and by cutting more jungle – made a Highway – a Super highway. She still goes back and forth on this road in her swanky high speed car driving or in a chauffeur driven car – She is a path breaker.

Having such a person as a friend, colleague, senior can do wonders. These informal Guides and mentors share their experiences of first time walk thru the jungle, the run on the Kuccha road – the rides in animal carts and the fast rides on the highway – all their work life experiences. They wizen the juniors and youngsters – such mentors are always in demand at the workplace.

One is lucky to have them.

Chapter Number 16

Forever Mentor
Choice of Mentors

"He was a kind, gracious, and generous friend, and a mentor beyond compare. "He was her friend and mentor until his death. Forever Mentor.

Chapter Number 17

Advisor and Mentor
Choice of Mentors

"He is our mentor, our guide, and he possesses an intellect the size of a planet". Advisor Mentor.

He was a Professor. He is a Scientist; she is the Key Note Speaker. She is a Winner of XYZ honor and a Padma Awardee. He is an Advisor to the Ministers. She advises Governments abroad.

We as students are in the awe of such people when then come to speak to us or when we hear them on TedX or Toastmasters. Some of them are extroverts and reach out, some are ambiverts still and need reaching out by us. The introverts among them need more effort to get under their skins.

But they are Great guides, Mentors due to their super intellect, special talent and can be of great help if and yes, IF only they take you under their wings not as Godfather/ Mother but as Mentee / Protégé'/ Protégée'.

The feeling is one of being on the 7th cloud or 9th and one feels you are on a very FAST TRACK in life but you are holding the finger of one of the greatest who would not let you fall, let you slip. This sheer feeling of Security and being in the company / aura of great people impacts a young mind and positively impacts their progress.

At one MSME meeting, I was speaking about similar efforts by Top businessmen and Automobile manufacturers who could choose among the 28000 odd MSME entrepreneurs all of them dealing in auto parts manufacturing. The need was felt that some of the better ones could do even more better if mentored by the Top businessmen who incidentally were Micro or Small businessman themselves once.

At the workplace, the Sales People throng the Senior who has a wonderful track record of closing sales / big deals as they wish to learn from their experiences – they wish to speak about their live difficulties and seek suggestions to deal with them.

Advisors and Mentors are two different people but very short term – with little possibility of building relationships – Celebrities and highly successful people can play the dual role well, if they choose to. Of course, the Mentee also need to make efforts at a convincing outreach.

Chapter Number 18

Performance Mentor
Choice of Mentors

 "A good mentor can help a Startup or Entrepreneur sort through the options and make decisions". Manage Mentor.

I was nearly on the verge of bankruptcy. My 6th and longest partnership was headed towards ruin. Two of my top customers had declared bankruptcy. One of them was an airline which owed me huge sum of money and the other a Telephone Directory publishing company.   My exporter clients were falling behind in payment. My Principals were talking of stopping business. My partner was not keen to fund further or stick thru but had spoken to couple of my friends that he wanted me out.

A friend once took me out. He said, I want you to meet someone. I thought he being an ex-CFO of a bank maybe he will suggest a financier or something. I went along. We reached a small bungalow with an open compound and no garden. In an ante-room which was barely 8X8 feet we entered on white mattress covered room which had the smell of incense sticks and some idols, flowers were kept neatly and a 4'tall Old man with a flowing beard in a clean white Dhoti-Kurta waited for us – or so it seemed.

As we entered, we were introduced by his nickname and he looked at me, looked at my forehead quickly and said "Your train has derailed Mr. Parkhe, good you came here, we shall pray together and get it back on Rails." We prayed. He then said, "Leave alone the business, get out of it as fast as possible – Pay off every debt by selling everything that you have, house, car, mobiles, scooter, gold every bank balance and come out of this clean. Forget about partnerships – resign from business, settle dues with your partner and if he wishes to continue leave everything to him. Do not ever think about this business or losses. Build a FORT in your MIND and do not let negative people and negative emotions near you, be very choosy about who you make friends with. In 6 month's time you will get a job – continue working there, if possible till you retire – don't look back. Pray and we shall know you are praying – we will pray from wherever we are."

I did exactly as he said. Got a job in a MNC where I worked for 17 years. Had sold off all my assets and paid every singer creditor and my partner. Life was back to normal soon and I did well in the career and retired. While doing this, I sometimes felt bad about the huge losses and wealth which I could never build back but I accepted this as what is fated for me and kept focus on my efforts in the job.

I never met the Saint again but spoke to him over phone whenever I could or when he called. These were courtesy calls to update how I am doing. He made decisions on my behalf without asking. TOLD me what to do and what not to do. Following that advice worked for me. Such Mentors are rare to come by in life.

In my lifetime I have been lucky to have found very able mentors and while do not wish to classify or grade/ rate them – I have tried to describe for the Startup / Entrepreneur / C-Level Executive what the mentors can do to add tremendous value to us and make us able to face the world in the face of success and failures.

One quote from Dr. Norman Vincent Peale is a short poem where he tells you to replace the name with your own "I have used Jay here which is my nick name" and use it when you are down, have failed a few times.

"Defeat does not Awe Jay,

Because he is on good terms

With Hope.

In the moments of Defeat

And Misery

He is looking forward

To Victory".

I never met Dr. Peale the Positive Thinking Guru but his books were my constant companions when I was down or had failed. His teaching of "Things average out, Good and bad days always come in equal proportion" are still fresh in my memory.

www.ingramcontent.com/pod-product-compliance
Lightning Source LLC
Chambersburg PA
CBHW041318180526
45172CB00004B/1150